myFocus READER

LEVEL F

Copyright © by Savvas Learning Company LLC. All Rights Reserved. Printed in the United States of America.

This publication is protected by copyright, and permission should be obtained from the publisher prior to any prohibited reproduction, storage in a retrieval system, or transmission in any form or by any means, electronic, mechanical, photocopying, recording, or otherwise. For information regarding permissions, request forms, and the appropriate contacts within the Savvas Learning Company Rights Management group, please send your query to the address below.

Savvas Learning Company LLC, 15 East Midland Avenue, Paramus, NJ 07652

Attributions of third party content appear on page 64, which constitutes an extension of this copyright page.

Savvas™ and **Savvas Learning Company™** are the exclusive trademarks of Savvas Learning Company LLC in the U.S. and other countries.

Savvas Learning Company publishes through its famous imprints **Prentice Hall®** and **Scott Foresman®** which are exclusive registered trademarks owned by Savvas Learning Company LLC in the U.S. and/or other countries.

Savvas Realize™ is the exclusive trademark of Savvas Learning Company LLC in the U.S. and/or other countries.

Unless otherwise indicated herein, any third party trademarks that may appear in this work are the property of their respective owners, and any references to third party trademarks, logos, or other trade dress are for demonstrative or descriptive purposes only. Such references are not intended to imply any sponsorship, endorsement, authorization, or promotion of Savvas Learning Company products by the owners of such marks, or any relationship between the owner and Savvas Learning Company LLC or its authors, licensees, or distributors.

ISBN-13: 978-0-328-99407-6
ISBN-10:   0-328-99407-3

9 23

Contents

Unit 1 Journeys 4

Sailing Solo Around the World 6

Travel for Science 8

A Visit to Ancient Lands 10

A New Life in a New Land 12

One Playground at a Time 14

Unit 2 Observations 16

The Ocean Explorer 18

Protecting Polar Bears 20

Wild Adventure in the Mountains 22

Our Wild Neighbors 24

Help for a Lonely Elephant 26

Unit 3 Reflections 28

A Fighter for Equal Rights 30

Helping Workers Reach Their Goals 32

Greek Mythology Today 34

Sharing Family Traditions 36

The Painters of Harlem 38

Unit 4 Liberty 40

Working Together for Survival 42

A Leader of the Underground Railroad 44

How We Protect Our Freedoms 46

She Fought for Women's Rights 48

A Better Life in Kansas 50

Unit 5 Systems 52

How Do Rocks Change? 54

How Water Changes Form 56

Struggles and Change for a Small Island Nation 58

Our Impact on the Life Cycle of Fish 60

Why Is Dog Training Important? 62

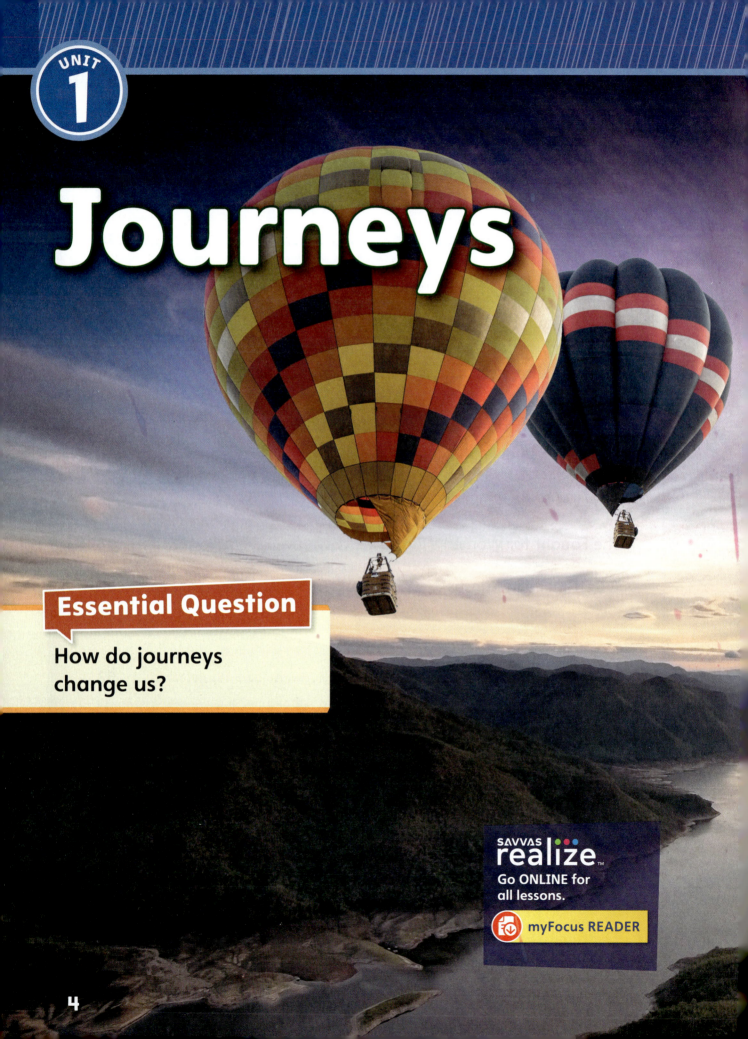

Read and Interact with Text
Develop comprehension and vocabulary. Make connections.

Sailing Solo Around the World
Weekly Question What motivates people to leave a place they call home?
Comprehension Text evidence
Academic Vocabulary Context clues

Travel for Science
Weekly Question What can scientists discover by traveling to distant places?
Comprehension Inferences
Academic Vocabulary Root words and affixes

A Visit to Ancient Lands
Weekly Question What can people learn from visiting unknown lands?
Comprehension Text evidence
Academic Vocabulary Context clues

A New Life in a New Land
Weekly Question What inspires people to start a journey?
Comprehension Visualization
Academic Vocabulary Context clues

One Playground at a Time
Weekly Question How can new places change the way a person sees the world?
Comprehension Predictions
Academic Vocabulary Shades of meaning

Sailing Solo Around the World

Imagine getting up one morning and having an idea to sail around the world alone. That was Jessica Watson's dream. She was a 16-year-old Australian girl. And she did it! On May 15, 2010, her 34-foot yacht named *Ella's Pink Lady* entered the harbor in Sydney, Australia. Her 23,000-mile adventure had started there. She sailed out of the same harbor 210 days earlier. As she crossed the finish line, Jessica became the youngest person to sail around the globe alone. She didn't stop. She didn't bring help.

Some did not recognize Jessica's voyage as a world record because of her age. Critics described her as reckless. They claimed that she shouldn't have been permitted to go. Others disagreed. Jessica had spent years training for and preparing for the risks and challenges. She and her family had cautiously planned the expedition. Jessica worked with an expert team to get her boat ready to sail across unpredictable oceans.

During the trip, Jessica was out of sight of land for months at a time. She had a satellite phone and could send and receive emails. She was alone except for dolphins, birds, and her "crew" of stuffed animals. However, she insists she never felt isolated. She was doing exactly what she wanted. She knew people all over the world were thinking about her.

Academic Vocabulary

There are three synonyms for *adventure* in this story. Go on a word search to find at least two of them.

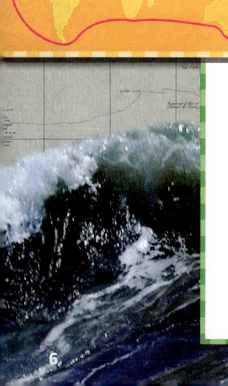

At one point, high winds shaped waves as tall as a four-story building. *Ella's Pink Lady* was knocked onto its side more than 6 times. Jessica said the boat was picked up and then thrown down a wave. The boat was forced under a mountain of breaking water. Then the boat violently turned upside down. Jessica had to strap herself into her bunk. She wore a crash helmet in the wild seas. She admits she sometimes questioned why she was making the trip. However, she always believed the challenges were worth it.

What gave Jessica such courage on her journey? She wanted to inspire people. She says she wanted to challenge herself and achieve something to be proud of. She hopes that by achieving her own dream, she is showing people that it is possible to reach their own goals. Jessica also wanted to prove her critics wrong. She says that part of what she's doing is proving that we shouldn't judge by appearance and our own expectations. She wants to give the world insight into exactly what 'little girls' and young people are actually capable of!

Analyze Main Ideas and Details

In this paragraph, there is a main idea and details. What is the main idea of this paragraph? What are the details?

Academic Vocabulary

The word *insight* contains the word "sight" which means "to see." How does knowing this help us understand the meaning of *insight*?

Unlock the Meaning of the Text

Use Text Evidence In the story, Jessica says she achieved her goals. What were her goals? Outline the steps she took that prove she achieved them.

Academic Vocabulary The word *insight* means "understanding." What clues in the text tell you what kind of insight Jessica wanted to give the world?

What motivates people to leave a place they call home? With a partner, discuss some of the reasons Jessica wanted to go on this journey. Then talk about your own journeys.

Travel for Science

Make Inferences
From reading the second and third paragraphs, what can you infer about what kind of person Charles Darwin was?

Have you ever wanted to learn about something you'd never seen before? It's hard to discover something in your own backyard. You already know what's there! Sometimes, scientists must travel a long distance to discover something new. Some even go halfway around the globe. Traveling to a mysterious place can open our eyes to new ideas and possibilities. We should keep an open mind like a scientist.

Charles Darwin was born in England in 1809. He went to medical school to become a doctor, but he didn't like it. He was too curious to stay inside all day. He wanted to explore new places and learn about nature. He loved being outside and observing plants and animals. He eventually became a naturalist, geologist, and biologist. He observed nature, Earth, and all the animals and plants that live here.

Darwin decided that he couldn't study and research animals and plants in England. There wasn't enough diversity there. He needed to go far away. When he was 22 years old, he set sail to South America on a vessel called the *HMS Beagle*. The journey began in 1831. The adventure would take five years.

The ship sailed along the west coast of South America. It stopped in a passage near an island archipelago just off the coast of Ecuador. These islands were called the Galapagos Islands. Darwin could not believe what he observed there. There were animals and plants he had never seen.

Academic Vocabulary
The word *passage* is the object of a preposition in this sentence.

They were perfectly adapted to their environments. The islands had been created from extinct volcanoes. So how did the animals get there? Darwin started thinking about the possibilities.

Because of his voyage to the Galapagos, Darwin had an **insightful** idea. He called it the theory of natural selection, or evolution. That meant humans were related to other animals, like fish and monkeys. Darwin believed that our bodies, over many generations, transformed to adapt to our environment. Eventually, we became the human beings we are now. In 1859, he wrote a book about the theory of evolution called *On the Origin of Species*.

Many people criticized Darwin's theory at the time. But now the theory of evolution is one of the most influential scientific theories of the modern era. If Charles Darwin had never decided to leave England for a remote, foreign land 6,000 miles away, the world would never have known about Darwin's grand idea.

Academic Vocabulary

Adding the suffix *-ful* to the word *insight* turns the noun into an adjective. What does the word *insightful* describe in this sentence?

Unlock the Meaning of the Text

Make Inferences Based on the third paragraph, what are some problems Darwin had before he went to the Galapagos? What did he need to do his work?

Academic Vocabulary The word *adventure* contains the Latin root "advenire," which means "to arrive." How does knowing that help you learn the definition of *adventure*?

What can scientists discover by traveling to distant places? With a partner, discuss why it was important to Darwin to leave England and travel to a distant place to make his discoveries.

A Visit to ANCIENT LANDS

Academic Vocabulary

A *passage* can be a long, narrow area, a section of a book, or a journey on a ship, among other things. How is the word used in this sentence?

Academic Vocabulary

The word *wandered* means "traveled slowly." How does removing the suffix *-ed* change the meaning of the word?

Let's take an adventure back in time. We'll travel more than 3,000 years ago to the west bank of the Nile River. Imagine building one of the many pyramids in the rocks of Egypt's Valley of the Kings. The laborers' work was difficult without metal tools. It could take many years to build the complex buildings. Most of them had stairs, rooms, and small passages.

The kings built pyramids as burial places for themselves and their families. The ancient Egyptians believed the soul lived on after death. They thought bodies needed to be kept whole to be in the afterlife. They thought the things a person had should be buried with the body. People hoping to steal gold and other treasures wandered into the pyramids over many years.

But in 1922, Howard Carter found a tomb that thieves had not seen. King Tut's burial room had not been seen for thousands of years. Most of the king's items were still there. So was his mummy. Carter also discovered four rooms filled with beautiful items. There were more than 5,000 objects. These included Tut's gold mask and throne. There were also jewelry, statues, and furniture. The discovery made a lot of people interested in ancient Egypt. It gave important clues to the lives of ancient Egyptians.

Now let's take another trip back in time. A city in the Andes Mountains of Peru was home to a great civilization. This was more than 500 years ago. Getting to the city was hard. The path was almost straight up in most places. Hiram Bingham heard about a "lost" city.

He was a historian. He led an adventure to the area in 1911.

Bingham noticed stairs on the mountain's sides. They were cut very nicely into rock. He found burial caves with skeletons and clay and stone pots. His men saw very old temples and houses. Machu Picchu was split into groups of homes with one entrance and a clever lock. People had cut the locks into granite using only very simple tools.

Machu Picchu was built in the fifteenth century. It was an emperor's vacation home. The city was an ideal place protected by nature. The city had a narrow passage on one side that connected it to another city. But the stairs were built to make it hard to attack. Bingham's group brought back thousands of items from the city. The treasures included skeletons, ceramic pottery, stoneware, bronze, and jewelry. These ancient items provide an interesting ==insight== into life in the Incan Empire when it was most powerful.

Understand Point of View

In this story, we learn about two ancient civilizations. Is the story written in first-person point of view or third-person point of view? How do you know?

Unlock the Meaning of the Text

Use Text Evidence In a group, make a chart comparing the two ancient civilizations the story talks about. What is similar about them? What is different?

Academic Vocabulary There are four vocabulary words in this story: *adventure*, *passages*, *wandered*, and *insight*. Write two sentences using two of the vocabulary words in each sentence.

What can people learn from visiting unknown lands? With a partner, discuss the journeys taken by Howard Carter and Hiram Bingham. What did they learn from their discoveries?

A New Life in a New Land

Academic Vocabulary

To *wander* means to "travel slowly." How does the phrase "through the streets" help you understand the meaning of *wander*?

"California is the most wonderful place on the Earth!" sang my father. We wandered through the winding, hilly streets of San Francisco.

I made a face. I had only been in California for a few hours, but already I was incredibly homesick for our village in China.

My mother said, "There is wealth everywhere and plenty of jobs to be had in California."

My father had traveled to America alone twice before. He had worked in factories and on the railroad. He had saved his earnings and wages. Now, our whole family had journeyed across the Pacific Ocean. We were to begin our adventure in a new land.

"You will like it here, Mei Li," added my mother.

I had lived in our town for my entire life, my whole ten years. How could I live without our little river or the rice fields? Or the beautiful Tree of Heaven outside our window? I had not seen a single Tree of Heaven in San Francisco.

"Life is better in America," my father explained as we crossed the dusty street. "China has famines and floods. Such disasters are almost unknown in California."

I thought he might be right, but it was crowded in California. There were strange people everywhere. They had too-pale skin and too-light hair. There were people who jabbered in a language I did not know. The houses looked uninviting. The air smelled different. How could I ever feel at home here? I was curious.

My father pointed, "That blue house is where I lived when I worked in the fish factory seven years ago. It will be our house now that we are immigrants to this land. It can never be the same as our house in China, but we will make it a home."

At first, I looked at the house and frowned. Then I had an insight. A tree that I knew well stood outside the blue house. "A Tree of Heaven!" I said, running to touch the familiar branches.

My father said, "Seven years ago, I took a seed from our Tree of Heaven in China. I brought it across the ocean and planted it here. I know how much you love that tree, Mei Li. This house could not be our home without a Tree of Heaven outside."

I breathed in the scent of the leaves, happier than I had been in weeks. "Thank you, Father," I said softly. I walked up to the house and opened the door to our new life.

Academic Vocabulary

In this sentence, the word *curious* can mean "eager to learn something" or "strange." Which meaning is the better fit in the story?

Visualize

In this story, Mei Li describes seeing the new Tree of Heaven. What words and phrases help you visualize what seeing the tree was like for her?

Unlock the Meaning of the Text

Visualize Mei Li describes San Francisco throughout the story. What words help you visualize what San Francisco looks like to her? How is it different from her village in China?

Academic Vocabulary Mei Li's family goes on a new *adventure* in this story. An *adventure* is a thrilling journey. What tells you that her new life is going to be an *adventure*?

What inspires people to start a journey? With a partner, discuss why Mei Li's father had come to California previously. Why did he want to move his family there?

ONE PLAYGROUND AT A TIME

Today was Aubrey's big day. It was her first time at the National Young Journalists' Conference. There were so many speakers she wanted to hear! Aubrey had spent a year sending her writing to magazines. But she had no success.

The conference was being held in the state capital. It was more than two hours away from Aubrey's house. She and her mother set out early that Saturday morning. They wanted to make sure they had plenty of time to get there. They would have, had their car not broken down.

When the engine came to a stop, Aubrey looked at her mom with tears in her eyes. She asked, "Will we be able to get to the conference on time?" Three phone calls later, Aubrey's mom broke the news that Aubrey feared. They would be very late to the conference. Aubrey was devastated. She muttered, "Why me? Why do I have such bad luck?"

As they waited for help, Aubrey's mom suggested they take a walk. Aubrey reluctantly agreed.

They wandered around the corner and reached a playground. This one was very different from the safe playground in the neighborhood park near their apartment. This playground was covered in cracked pavement that looked dangerous. Two of the three swings were broken. Only one of the seesaws had boards. Aubrey noticed the rusty slide and the

Make and Confirm Predictions

At the end of the second paragraph, the story changes direction. How do you know the story is not going to be about the journalism conference?

Academic Vocabulary

The word *wandered* has the suffix *-ed*. What does the suffix tell us about the meaning of the root word *wander*?

splintered wood on the benches. The basketball court had broken backboards with no hoops.

Aubrey was sad but was suddenly inspired. She and her mom hurried to the car to get Aubrey's notebook and camera. Aubrey interviewed several people when she returned to the playground. She talked to the kids and their parents. She was curious about how much time they would be willing to donate to fix this place up if she could find the money to do it. She wrote down their ideas about new equipment. Everyone seemed excited to help.

Aubrey started a campaign to fix old and damaged playgrounds all over the county after that. She wrote opinion articles in the newspaper. With the help of community leaders, she made calls. Aubrey planned fundraisers and community workdays. She called for volunteers.

That was six years ago. Today, Aubrey is getting ready to start her senior year. She's about to begin fixing up her seventh playground. If you ask her how she got started with this project, she begins her answer by saying, "Well, actually it was a matter of luck."

Academic Vocabulary

The word *curious* means both "eager to know something" and "strange." Which definition fits this sentence best?

Unlock the Meaning of the Text

Make and Confirm Predictions Aubrey thought the car breaking down was bad luck. Did you think the story would have a sad or happy ending after that? Were you right?

How can new places change the way a person sees the world? In a group, discuss how Aubrey's point of view changed from the beginning of the story to the end. Discuss how seeing new places has changed how you see the world.

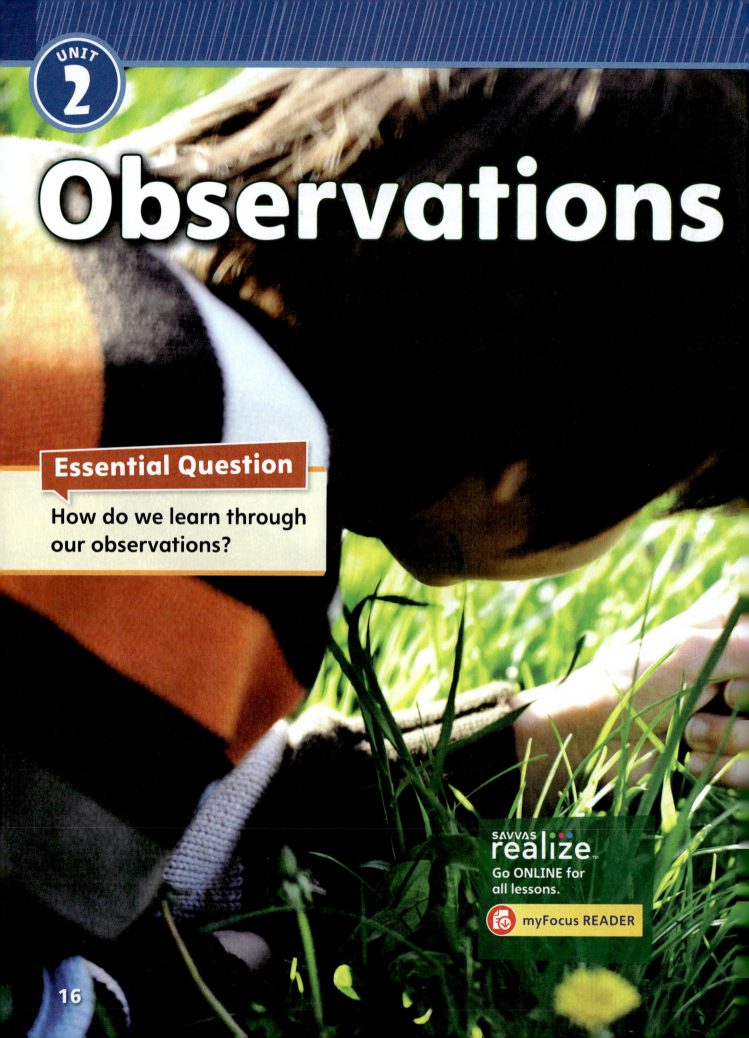

Read and Interact with Text
Develop comprehension and vocabulary. Make connections.

The Ocean Explorer
Weekly Question Why do scientists explore and study oceans?
Comprehension Details
Academic Vocabulary Shades of meaning

Protecting Polar Bears
Weekly Question What can people do to protect species from a changing environment?
Comprehension Text structure
Academic Vocabulary Root words and affixes

Wild Adventure in the Mountains
Weekly Question How can careful observation help a person survive?
Comprehension Point of view
Academic Vocabulary Root words and affixes

Our Wild Neighbors
Weekly Question What can we learn from studying animals in their natural habitats?
Comprehension Text ideas
Academic Vocabulary Context clues

Help for a Lonely Elephant
Weekly Question What are some different ways in which people can observe and protect wildlife?
Comprehension Information
Academic Vocabulary Context clues

THE OCEAN EXPLORER

Academic Vocabulary

The word *focus* can be used as both a noun and a verb. Which part of speech is this use of the word *focus*?

It seemed that almost the entire world had been explored by the middle of the 1900s. Adventurers had climbed Mount Everest. They had visited the South Pole and the North Pole. They had explored the densest forests and the driest deserts on Earth. It was not a great time for a person to try to make a name for himself as an explorer. But Jacques-Yves Cousteau (coo-STOH) was not worried that almost every spot on dry land had already been visited by someone. Cousteau decided to focus on what many considered the last unexplored part of Earth. He explored the oceans.

Cousteau was born in France in 1910. He began studying the oceans around 1936. Over the next few years, he did a lot of deep-sea diving. In 1943, he dove about 59 feet into the ocean. He made a short film about what the world looked like that deep. A few years later, Cousteau helped develop better and more reliable gear for underwater travel. He helped make it possible for adventurers like himself to spend more and more time under the water.

Academic Vocabulary

The verb *detect* is related to the noun *detective*. Can you identify how the two words are related based on the definition of *detect*?

Between the 1950s and 1970s, Cousteau made several studies about the oceans and marine life. For example, he would detect shipwrecks and study them closely. He also made some important discoveries regarding porpoises and their use of sonar to navigate. He also talked about environmental awareness. He encouraged people not to pollute the oceans.

18

Cousteau invented several machines and vehicles that could travel deeper into the ocean. In 1956, he built a dish-shaped vehicle that could reach 1,148 feet deep. Ten years later, he designed another. This one traveled 1,640 feet (500 m) deep. Cousteau filmed the oceans while he was underwater. He later shared the films with people around the world. His work greatly increased knowledge of the oceans and what lives there.

Through his work, he became famous. But scientists also argued about his work. Some said that he was too interested in making the oceans popular. They thought he was not interested enough in studying them. An oceanographer is an expert who studies the oceans. Cousteau was not a trained oceanographer. Because of that, some say he sometimes made scientific ideas too simple in his books, films, and lectures. But Cousteau remains famous today for his work. He died in 1997 after a long life of adventure.

Evaluate Details

With a partner, make an outline of the details from the story about Jacques Cousteau. Include details about both his life and work.

Unlock the Meaning of the Text

Evaluate Details Review the list you made with your partner. Pick out three details from your list you think are most important about Cousteau's life and work.

Academic Vocabulary The word *expert* means both "a person who has knowledge" and "skillful." Which definition fits better in the last paragraph where *expert* is used?

Why do scientists explore and study oceans? With a partner, go through the story and identify some of Cousteau's main discoveries. What did Cousteau find so exciting about the oceans?

PROTECTING POLAR BEARS

Want to adopt a polar bear? Now you can! The bear won't really live with you of course. That's because polar bears spend most of their lives on the frozen Arctic sea ice. They are the largest land mammal that needs the sea to live. Polar bears are important predators in the Arctic's marine food chain. And their health shows the health of the whole ecosystem. Sadly, changes in the environment now relate to problems for these amazing animals. For example, there are now 20 percent fewer polar bears in northern Canada than there were in the 1990s.

Changes in the environment include rising temperatures. This has caused there to be less sea ice. Sea ice forms on the water's surface when salt water freezes. Polar bears need the sea ice to breed and rest. They also use it as a good spot to detect prey. Seals are the bears' favorite thing to hunt. Seals must often come to the surface for air. Bears wait at openings in the ice where the seals come to breathe. Now, seals can surface anywhere because melting sea ice has left large patches of open water. That makes it more difficult for the bears to find their main source of food.

In the past, bears looking for food could travel a long way. They could just walk across the sea ice. They might sometimes swim a short distance between ice

Academic Vocabulary

The word *relate* means "to make a connection." In this sentence, what two ideas does the word *relate* connect?

Academic Vocabulary

The word *detect* means "to find." Now that you know the definition, name some synonyms for the word *detect*.

blocks. Now they have to swim much farther. Sometimes they might spend the summers without enough food. In this case, they live off the fat in their bodies. This is especially true for females with cubs. The cubs might not be strong enough for long swims. They still rely on their mothers for food. Many polar bears might be malnourished. They might even starve because of this.

Concerned scientists, experts, and volunteers from conservation organizations like the World Wildlife Fund (WWF) and Polar Bear International are working hard to assist polar bears. They learn more about polar bear habits by tracking individual animals. They ask for help from native people who have lived with these animals and respect them. The WWF works to protect endangered places. The organization tries to limit oil and gas drilling. These are threats to the environment and to the bears' habitats. The WWF also raises money. It asks people to donate money to "adopt" an animal. This helps pay for research.

Conservation organizations need all the help they can get. Check out ways you can help protect polar bears without even leaving your home!

Analyze Text Structure

The end of the text is a "call to action," meaning it is asking you to do something. What is the text asking you to do?

Unlock the Meaning of the Text

Analyze Text Structure The text has three main ideas. What is the main idea of the first paragraph? The second and third paragraphs? The fourth and fifth paragraphs?

Academic Vocabulary The word *expert* comes from the Latin root "experiri," which means "to try." How does knowing that help us understand the definition of *expert*?

What can people do to protect a species from a changing environment? With a partner, talk about the ways the WWF helps to protect polar bears. What can you do to help?

Wild Adventure in the Mountains

Analyze Point of View

Is this story written in first- or third-person point of view? What words tell you?

Caroline's mom and dad had adored the outdoors for as long as she could remember. This year, the whole family was going on a weeklong vacation. They would stay in the Adirondack Mountains. They rented a cabin deep in the woods. Their plans were to hike the Adirondacks, swim in the lake, and catch fish for dinner.

As they got close to the cabin, Caroline pointed out an old sign alongside the road. The sign said, "Welcome to Bear Country." She asked her father what this meant. He explained that the Adirondack Mountains were home to both vacationers and to black bears. Her father said these fierce predators are just about as frightened of people as people are afraid of them. "However," he told Caroline in a solemn voice, "mother black bears can be aggressive. They will do anything to protect their cubs. If you are ever between a black bear and her cubs, slowly and quietly retreat. Don't make eye contact with the bear."

Caroline was thrilled when she thought about seeing a bear. But she was also a little concerned about getting too close to one of the gigantic animals. Caroline was certain this was going to turn out to be an exciting vacation.

Caroline was not disappointed. On their second hike, she saw a small bear about twenty feet away. The bear was just to the right of the narrow trail. Caroline breathed sharply.

Then she stood still where she was. She tugged on her father's sleeve, then heard a threatening howl coming from the left. Momma Bear had spotted the hikers. They were visible to her directly in between her and her cub. She snuffed and snorted. The colossal bear started to paw the ground. She pounced on her front paws, threatening to charge toward the family.

Caroline's first instinct was to run. Her father must have detected this. He placed his hand on Caroline's shoulder and whispered, "Remember what I told you." They kept their eyes focused on the ground and began inching calmly back down the trail. Within minutes, the mother bear was reunited with her cub, and they disappeared into the trees.

"Wow! That was close and a little scary!" Caroline exclaimed. Her mother agreed but added, "Can you blame a mother for protecting her babies? That's just how I acted when you were that age." They all laughed thinking about Caroline's mother snorting and pawing the ground to protect Caroline.

Academic Vocabulary
The word *visible* comes from the Latin root "videre" meaning "to see." How does knowing that help us understand the definition of *visible*?

Academic Vocabulary
A synonym for the word *focused* is "concentrated." What other synonyms for *focused* can you name?

Unlock the Meaning of the Text

Analyze Point of View With a partner, identify whose point of view the story is told from. How would the story be different if it was told in first-person?

Academic Vocabulary In this story, the word *detected* has the suffix -*ed*. How does this suffix affect the meaning of the word *detect* in the story?

How can careful observation help a person survive? In a small group, discuss Caroline's observations when she was hiking. How did her observations help her learn what to do in that situation?

Our Wild Neighbors

Today many people live in homes in spots where animals once lived in peace. Some people like their visible animal neighbors. They may like watching deer or birds in their backyard. Others see animals as unwanted and annoying. Either way, more humans are moving into animal areas. You can't avoid contact between people and wild animals. But humans must be willing to change some of their habits.

Birds are a good example. They often fly toward the bright lights of tall city buildings. But the lights can disturb the birds' migration path. Some become tired and confused. Some birds will circle the buildings over and over. Because of this, the birds are late to their migration. This makes it more likely that they won't live through winter storms before getting to where they're going. Some cities, such as Chicago, have started volunteer Lights Out programs. Buildings lower or turn off their lights between 11 p.m. and sunrise during the times when the birds migrate.

Lights on beaches are related to wildlife, too. Newly hatched sea turtles wait below the sand until dark. They are led to the sea by both nature and how bright the sky is over the water. Sometimes, newly hatched turtles will see lights on the beach. If this happens, they may move toward the lights and away from the water. They need water, and there isn't any on land. One idea is to turn the lights off or make them lower during the weeks when the turtle eggs hatch. Another is to aim the lights straight down.

Academic Vocabulary

What word in the third sentence of the first paragraph gives you the best idea of what the word *visible* means?

Academic Vocabulary

With a group, discuss what two things are connected based on the use of the word *related*, which means "connected."

Deer, opossums, and raccoons can do a lot of harm to gardens and homes. Deer will eat a lot of different plants. But a fence or bright lights that turn on when something moves may keep them away. People who own houses should trim trees. This can stop opossums and raccoons from jumping onto a roof and getting into an attic. Keeping garbage cans tightly closed is a good way to stop raccoons, coyotes, and red foxes. People also shouldn't leave food outside for their pets. It may attract wildlife. More than birds are interested in what's inside a bird feeder.

Some people support catching and moving unwanted animals. But this often doesn't work. Studies by experts show that more than half of the animals that are moved to another area won't survive in these new places. Nobody says it will always be easy, but learning how to live with wild animals might be a better idea.

Explain Ideas in Texts

The last paragraph tells us we should learn to live with animals. What ideas in the story tell us how to do that?

Unlock the Meaning of the Text

Explain Ideas in Texts Take turns explaining to a partner why birds and turtles are affected by what humans do and what we can do to help, based on the text.

Academic Vocabulary In the text, *experts* tell us important information. Why are *experts* important to listen to? How does the definition of *expert* help us know that?

What can we learn from studying animals in their natural habitats? With a partner, list all the things in the text we've learned from watching animals. Then, discuss the problems for each animal group (birds, turtles, other wild animals).

HELP FOR A LONELY ELEPHANT

Every morning, Olivia hurried to clean cages at the zoo's monkey habitat. As she did, she passed by the small elephant enclosure where Kabanda lived. Often, she heard him speaking to her as she passed. He usually made a soft rumbling sound that Olivia was certain meant, "I'm lonely."

Olivia understood that elephants are very social animals. Kabanda had been all alone in his enclosure for almost two years, ever since his mate Adana had died. So, every morning, Olivia made sure she responded to the pachyderm in her most soothing voice. "I know, Kabanda, I know," she said.

Some mornings, Olivia noticed Kabanda moved back and forth a little and bobbed his head. She knew this behavior was common in elephants that remained in cages for a long time. She had read articles by experts about how elephants began to show signs of sadness or depression. Olivia would tell Kabanda, "So many people care about you. Change is coming, Kabanda!"

And it was. Olivia was not the only one who related to the huge animal alone in the tiny space. Kabanda had been in the news ever since his companion had died. The zoo where he lived and Olivia worked was old. It had been constructed before people fully understood or sympathized with the needs of animals in captivity.

Academic Vocabulary

The word *experts* in the third paragraph is plural. How do you know? Find other plural words in this story.

Academic Vocabulary

The word *related* means both "connected to" and "identified with." Which meaning best fits the use in this sentence?

People had serious concerns about the zoo's elephant enclosure because many people now believe that elephants need lots of natural space. They need acres and acres of land. However, Kabanda was stuck in just a half-acre or so. Kabanda sometimes made a loud trumpeting sound. Some zoo visitors related this to a cry of misery. Others said that there was no such thing as a decent zoo for elephants. They said that elephants need entire wildlife parks. They need a place where several animal families can roam around and find their own food.

Kabanda never got to live in a wildlife park. But his grief at the old zoo didn't last much longer. One morning, Olivia stopped at his enclosure. She pointed west beyond the city borders. She said, "Kabanda, I have incredible news for you. You're moving to a new zoo over that hill. It's much bigger, and best of all, there are other elephants. You will not be alone." Of course, Olivia knew that Kabanda couldn't understand what she was saying. Kabanda suddenly lifted his head and trumpeted. Olivia wondered if maybe he understood her after all.

Synthesize Information

With a partner, explain how what happens in the fourth and fifth paragraphs leads to what happens in the sixth paragraph.

Unlock the Meaning of the Text

Synthesize Information In the third paragraph, we learn information about elephants. How does that information tell us what needs to change for Kabanda?

Academic Vocabulary In the fourth paragraph, the word *related* connects two ideas. Which two ideas in the paragraph does the word *related* connect?

What are some ways people can observe and protect wildlife? With a group, discuss how Olivia's research helped her relate to Kabanda. What kind of research about animals can you do?

UNIT 3

Reflections

Essential Question

How do experiences of others reflect our own?

Read and Interact with Text
Develop comprehension and vocabulary. Make connections.

A Fighter for Equal Rights

Weekly Question What can we learn from the experiences of older generations?

Comprehension Connections

Academic Vocabulary Shades of meaning

Helping Workers Reach Their Goals

Weekly Question What are some different ways in which people can reach a goal?

Comprehension Summarize plot

Academic Vocabulary Shades of meaning

Greek Mythology Today

Weekly Question How are the experiences of people in ancient times similar to those of people in the modern world?

Comprehension Information

Academic Vocabulary Part of speech

Sharing Family Traditions

Weekly Question What can our families teach us about ourselves?

Comprehension Visualization

Academic Vocabulary Context clues

The Painters of Harlem

Weekly Question How does art reflect people's experiences?

Comprehension Predictions

Academic Vocabulary Synonyms

A Fighter for Equal Rights

Academic Vocabulary

The word *recall* has the prefix *re-*, which means "again." How does knowing that help us understand the definition of *recall* in this sentence?

President Barack Obama gave a speech in honor of educator and social activist Dr. Dorothy Height on April 29, 2010. He praised her. He recalled her life as "a life that lifted other lives; a life that changed this country for the better over the course of nearly one century here on Earth." Below is a summary of that speech.

Progress came from the group effort of many generations of Americans. From preachers and lawyers, and thinkers and doers. Men and women like Dr. Height took it upon themselves to change this country for the better. Often they did this at great risk . . . Well, Dr. Dorothy Height deserves this honor. She deserves a place in our history books. She also deserves a place of honor in America's memory.

Academic Vocabulary

The word *confide* comes from the Latin root "confidere," which means "to trust." How does knowing the root help us understand the definition of *confide*?

Look at the work she did. She desegregated the YWCA. She laid the foundation for integration on Wednesdays in Mississippi. Lending pigs to poor farmers as a helpful source of income. She confided in civil rights leaders. She was often the only woman in the room. Height was like a Queen Esther to this Moses Generation. Even as she led the National Council of Negro Women with vision and class.

But we remember her not only for all she did during the civil rights movement. We remember her for all she did over a lifetime. We remember all she did behind the scenes so the movement would reach more people. To shine a light on stable families and close communities. Her <mark>perspective</mark> was that civil rights and women's rights were not separate struggles but parts of a larger movement. This movement was to secure the rights of all humanity. It didn't matter what a person's gender, race, or ethnicity was.

It's a clear record of good work. It is worthy of remembering, worthy of recognition. And yet, funny enough, year after year for many decades, Dr. Height went about her work quietly. She didn't need fanfare or self-promotion. She never cared about who got the credit. She didn't need to see her picture in the papers. She understood that the movement gathered strength from the bottom up. Some men and women don't always make it into the history books. But they always insisted on their dignity, their manhood and womanhood. She wasn't interested in credit. What she cared about was the cause. The cause of justice. The cause of equality. The cause of opportunity.

Make Connections

How do President Obama's comments help us learn about Dr. Height as a person? Which comments in this paragraph are the most helpful?

Unlock the Meaning of the Text

Make Connections Make a chart with two columns. Label one column "Life," and label the other column "Work." Fill in the chart with details from the text about Dr. Height's life and work.

Academic Vocabulary The word *perspective* has two meanings: One deals with art, and the other deals with how we see the world. Which meaning fits best in the fourth paragraph?

What can we learn from the experiences of older generations? With a partner, talk about Dr. Height's experiences from the text. What did you learn about how life was different for Dr. Height's generation?

Helping Workers Reach Their Goals

Sequence of Events
Work with a partner and identify the events that took place in the first paragraph. Put the events in order.

Academic Vocabulary
The word *perspective* comes from the Latin root *spectere*, which means "to look." How does that help us understand the meaning of *perspective* in this sentence?

Look in a bathroom sink or bathtub. You might see the name Kohler on it. In the late 1800s, John Michael Kohler came to America from Austria. He started the Kohler Company in Sheboygan, Wisconsin. The company became known for the very good bathroom products it made. The business grew very fast. One of the products people liked most were bathtubs designed like what farm animals drink from. Eventually the Sheboygan factory became too small. A new factory was built in the country four miles away. After the death of John Michael Kohler and two of his sons, another son, Walter, took charge. The company wanted to demonstrate that it wanted to make its workers' lives better. Many of the workers came from Austria.

The Kohler Company made sure workers were safe. They made sure their workers could see a doctor. They paid them more than other businesses. Not every business in the Midwest did this. Walter Kohler had a different perspective. He wanted to make sure his employees worked in a nice place. He also wanted to make sure their homes were nice, too. He did not want the growing town around the factory to have too many people or to be an ugly city. Kohler liked what he saw in other cities in the United States and Europe. He talked with the best architects and planners. Then, he started turning the Village of Kohler into one of the first planned communities in the Midwest.

The town had many ==appealing== features. There were parks, different kinds of homes, areas for fun, and a school. Creating a company town helped the business find and keep the best workers. It also provided help to employees. Because of Walter Kohler, the company built the American Club. This was a place where immigrant workers could live. It was cheap to live there. Workers usually paid less than $30 a month. Many Kohler workers who weren't married stayed there. Then, they saved enough to buy a house and send for their families. Workers took lessons in English. They learned American history and civics. Immigrant workers got a day off and transportation to the courthouse as a first step toward becoming citizens.

When the American Club was completed in 1918, a company newsletter called it an important building for democracy. Between 1900 and 1930, the Kohler Company helped at least 1,200 immigrant workers become citizens. A person who wrote about Walter Kohler said that the American Club was where people came to be Americans.

Academic Vocabulary

When we add the suffix *-ing* to the word *appeal*, it becomes an adjective meaning "attractive or interesting." What other synonyms can you think of for *appealing*?

Unlock the Meaning of the Text

Sequence of Events Complete the list of events you made for the first paragraph for the rest of the story. How did the Kohler Company change from when it was first founded?

Academic Vocabulary The word *demonstrate* could mean "prove something by giving evidence" or "show by one's actions." Which meaning is the best use in the first paragraph?

What are some different ways in which people can reach a goal? In a small group, discuss Walter Kohler's goal. Discuss his workers' goals. What are some ways Kohler and his workers both reached their goals?

Greek Mythology Today

Academic Vocabulary

The word *appeal* means both "make an urgent request" and "be attractive." Which meaning fits best in the first sentence of this paragraph?

If you think the appeal of ancient Greece ended long ago, think again. Those Greeks just won't leave us alone. Or maybe it's the other way around! We all know that the stories from ancient Greece had a big effect on our lives. But did you know that names from Greek mythology are still in our life today in many ways? You can find them in places from sports to spacecraft to companies and brands.

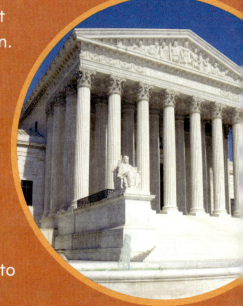

Many ancient Greek gods and warriors were very powerful. So it's not surprising that we see their names in sports teams. Greek stories say titans created the whole universe and all the less powerful gods. So it makes sense that Tennessee football owners might name a team the Tennessee Titans. (By the way, the New York Jets used to be the New York Titans before they changed their name to something more modern.) Why does Michigan State University call its team the Spartans? The Spartans came from Sparta, an area of Greece. They demonstrated that they were very good at war. They trained the kind of army that often won.

Academic Vocabulary

In this sentence, the word *demonstrated* means "showed." What are some other synonyms for *demonstrated*?

Greek names are not just in sports. Scientists at the National Aeronautics and Space Administration (NASA) have also used Greek names. The Apollo space program was named after the god of the sun. Apollo drove his chariot across the sky. The Gemini program was named after a pair of twins from Greek myths. The Poseidon and Trident missiles were named after the Greek god of the sea and his three-pronged spear. A military group named some large planes Hercules. They probably thought about the amazing Greek who was very strong.

You might recall an online store named after the giant Amazon River. Spanish explorers named that river. They had probably heard of the Amazons. These were a group of powerful women warriors from Greek mythology. You may have also heard of the moving company named after Atlas. This was the god who carried the world on his back.

Do a little research. You may be surprised to discover many products and businesses named for figures in Greek mythology. Ajax, Orion, Oracle, Pandora, and Midas are all from Greek mythology and have new meanings to us today. Greeks are everywhere!

Synthesize Information

Based on the text, what characteristics of Greek culture and mythology can you identify that are so appealing to us in modern times?

Unlock the Meaning of the Text

Synthesize Information On one side of a sheet of paper, write each example of how modern people have used Greek names. On the other, write the characteristics they wanted to portray through their naming.

Academic Vocabulary The word *recall* is both a noun and a verb. Which part of speech for the word *recall* is used in the first sentence of the fourth paragraph?

How are the experiences of people in ancient times similar to those of people in the modern world? With a partner, find adjectives in the text that describe you or your friends and family. How are the ancient Greeks similar to you?

Sharing Family Traditions

Jose Fernandez immigrated to the United States with his family when he was three years old. His only noticeable Latino features were his name and the little bit of Spanish he spoke when his grandmother visited each year. She lived in Puerto Rico. Jose had not been back to Puerto Rico. He didn't know much about his family's history.

That partly explains why he wasn't excited when he found out his school was going to have a multicultural festival. It would be on the first Saturday in March. "Boring!" Jose muttered. The school principal explained the festival. He said he needed students to organize booths for different countries. "So there will be three or four booths in the gym," Jose thought. "But what will we do there for a whole day?"

"Students, this will be a fun project," the principal said. "I think you all will learn a lot."

Mr. Li, the sixth-grade teacher, explained that the booths could have food and music. They could also demonstrate crafts from each country. Jose started to be interested. Everyone began making plans. Students began to talk about where they were from and different cultures. Patrick said he would organize the Ireland booth. David announced that his father moved here from Kenya. Cheena's family was from Northern India. Katuk was from Bali. The excitement Jose's classmates had for their own cultures was spreading. "I can run the booth for Puerto Rico!" Jose exclaimed.

Visualize

After reading about some of the students' backgrounds, can you visualize what their booths might look like?

When Jose came home, he asked his dad if he could call his grandmother to get ideas for the booth. His dad agreed, but he also volunteered to help Jose himself. "You know," he confided, "I grew up in Puerto Rico, so I know a lot about the culture and the history. So does your mom." Jose nodded when his dad suggested going through old family recipes to find something to cook for the festival.

Jose worked hard for a month making posters and maps. He gathered materials for his booth. His was one of the most appealing and interactive of all the booths. Jose beamed as everyone tried the guava pudding. They listened to salsa music and shook the maracas he and his dad had made. The principal had been right. The festival was a lot of fun. Jose had learned about different cultures. But perhaps more importantly, he learned about his own.

Academic Vocabulary

The Latin root of the word *confide* is "confidere," which means "to trust." How does knowing this help us define *confide* in terms of this sentence?

Academic Vocabulary

The word *appealing* also means "interesting" or "attractive." What other synonyms for *appealing* can you name?

Unlock the Meaning of the Text

Visualize Read the last paragraph. Can you visualize what Jose's booth looked like? Discuss with a partner the sounds, smells, and tastes of the Puerto Rico booth.

Academic Vocabulary In the fourth paragraph, paraphrase the sentence with the word *demonstrate* to show you know the meaning of the word.

What can our families teach us about ourselves? With a partner, make a list of the things Jose learned about his family from making his booth. What has your family background taught you about yourself?

The Painters of Harlem

In the 1920s and 1930s, many African American artists, writers, and musicians moved to New York City. They joined other African Americans in a neighborhood called Harlem. Many African Americans moved from southern states. They wanted to build a new life. Northern cities like New York and Boston had different jobs. Cities also offered a better life for their families.

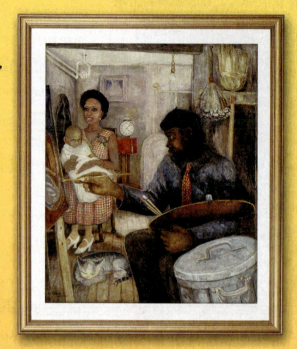

In the South, African Americans left jobs as servants or as farm workers. In the North, they found higher-paying jobs in factories. Some were teachers. Many found what they were looking for in New York City. Harlem became a busy and lively place. There was a lot of inspiration for artists and writers.

Harlem soon had the most African Americans in the United States. African American art, music, and literature had wide appeal. This time became known as the Harlem Renaissance.

This time in history is most famous for literature and music. Jazz musicians like Bessie Smith and Billie Holiday sang beautiful songs. Louis Armstrong played the trumpet like no one had ever heard before. Writers like Zora Neale Hurston and Langston Hughes wrote about how African Americans lived in cities and in the country. They demonstrated what life was like for African Americans during that time.

Academic Vocabulary

The word *appeal* means "interesting" or "attractive." Use other synonyms for *appeal* to describe Harlem based on your reading.

Make and Confirm Predictions

After reading about what the famous writers wrote about during this time period, what predictions can you make about the artists of this time?

However, art was also important during that time. Painters showed real African American life and culture. Paintings showed what life was like for African Americans in American cities. These artists painted from their own perspective.

Palmer Hayden was an important African American artist. He was one of the first to paint African Americans. Hayden painted real people in both northern cities and the southern countryside. He painted people in everyday scenes. One of his paintings is called *The Janitor Who Paints*. It shows a woman and her child having their picture painted.

Laura Wheeler Waring was a portrait painter. Her best-known portraits were of famous people of the Harlem Renaissance. She painted the writer James Weldon Johnson. She also painted the opera singer Marian Anderson.

Art from the Harlem Renaissance shows how the African American population changed. It shows the move of many African Americans from the country in the South to cities in the North. It shows how African American culture had an impact on Harlem and on the rest of the country.

Academic Vocabulary

The word *perspective* contains the phoneme *spec* which means "to look." How does this help you understand the meaning of *perspective*?

Unlock the Meaning of the Text

Make and Confirm Predictions After reading the title, predict what the text is going to be about. After you have finished reading, explain whether your predictions were correct.

Academic Vocabulary The word *demonstrate* means "to show." Do a word search and find other synonyms for *demonstrate* in the text.

How does art reflect people's experiences? In a small group, make a list of the artists, writers, and musicians mentioned in the text. How did their art reflect their experiences?

UNIT 4
Liberty

Essential Question

What does it mean to be free?

Read and Interact with Text
Develop comprehension and vocabulary. Make connections.

Working Together for Survival
Weekly Question Why should people work together to help others achieve freedom?
Comprehension Details
Academic Vocabulary Synonyms

A Leader of the Underground Railroad
Weekly Question How can ordinary people contribute to a fight for freedom?
Comprehension Comprehension
Academic Vocabulary Synonyms

How We Protect Our Freedoms
Weekly Question What can governments do to protect our freedoms?
Comprehension Summary
Academic Vocabulary Context clues

She Fought for Women's Rights
Weekly Question What are some things people can do when their freedom is limited?
Comprehension Question
Academic Vocabulary Meaning relationships

A Better Life in Kansas
Weekly Question How can going to a new place give a person new opportunities?
Comprehension Inferences
Academic Vocabulary Synonyms

WORKING TOGETHER FOR SURVIVAL

On August 5, 2010, workers arrived at the San José (san hoh-ZAY) mine in northern Chile (CHILL-ee) to start their workday. One group of miners traveled deep into the mine. They used a spiraling ramp. The miners began digging for copper and gold about 2,300 (701 m) feet beneath the surface. August 5 seemed like an ordinary day on the job for them.

It wasn't. The ramp's ceiling unexpectedly collapsed that afternoon. No one died in the cave-in. But tons of rock and soil now blocked the miners' only way out. These 33 men were trapped deep underground.

The men knew that their only hope was to wait for help to come. They also knew that rescue might be a long time coming. It might not come at all. The miners rationed their food carefully because of that. Each man got a few bites of tuna and cracker each day and not much else. The men also tried to develop routines. They tried to stay fit by walking through unblocked tunnels.

Seventeen days passed. They had less and less food. Conditions became worse. Some miners grew depressed. They worried they would never be found. But help came. A small drill broke through the roof of the mine on August 22. It was a probe. Rescue workers on the surface were trying to find the men. The hole was only six inches (15 cm) across. It was a little bigger than a grapefruit. The miners attached a note to the drill that said, "We are well in the shelter."

Evaluate Details

From the details you read in the first two paragraphs, what can you evaluate about the miners' situation? What do you think will happen?

The rescuers were amazed when they pulled the drill back up. They felt empowered. No one thought that the miners would still be alive. The rescuers quickly began digging a tunnel large enough to bring up the miners. They used the existing hole to send down food, medicine, lights, and communication devices. The miners grew more hopeful. They also were more emotional as their situation continued.

For weeks, rescuers drilled through the rock. They drilled as quickly as possible and made a steel rescue capsule to carry the workers to safety. More than two months after the collapse, everything was ready for the rescue attempt. Over the course of the next 24 hours, beginning on October 12, the capsule traveled again and again down the mine tunnel. Each time the capsule came back up with a miner inside. Finally, after 69 days underground, all 33 men were safe. The world watched and applauded the miners and the noble rescue workers who never gave up.

Unlock the Meaning of the Text

Evaluate Details With a partner, make a timeline showing all the events from August 5 through October 12. How does knowing the order of the events help you understand the story?

Academic Vocabulary The word *noble* might make you think of royalty. How does that help you understand the definition of *noble* in the sixth paragraph?

Why should people work together to help others achieve freedom? With a partner, make a list of the ways the rescuers helped the miners and the ways the miners helped the rescuers. Discuss why we should work together.

Academic Vocabulary

The word *empower* means both "give someone power" and "make confident." Which definition is the best fit for the word's use in this sentence?

Academic Vocabulary

The word *noble* is both an adjective and a noun. Which part of speech is used in this sentence for the word *noble*?

A Leader of the Underground Railroad

In 1850, people could own other people in the United States. Enslaved people were possessions. Slave owners could buy and sell a person for as much as $3,000. For this reason, slave owners offered rewards for the capture of escaped slaves.

The Underground Railroad was a secret network of people. This brave group resisted slavery. They risked the consequences of breaking the law to help people escape slavery. The enslaved people they helped made their way to northern states or to Canada. Slavery was outlawed there. The group used railroad words to help keep their activities secret. *Stations* were homes of families who would feed and hide the fugitives. The routes between the stations were called *lines*. *Conductors* guided runaways from one station to another. The enslaved people being transported were called *packages* or *freight*.

Both sympathetic white people and free African Americans participated in the Underground Railroad. But one of the best-known conductors had escaped slavery herself. Harriet Tubman was born into slavery in Maryland around 1820. Tubman made the decision to escape by the fall of 1849. She would prefer to die if she could not have freedom. A gracious white

Academic Vocabulary

The word *resist* means "to prevent yourself from being forced to do something." How did the Underground Railroad resist slavery?

Monitor Comprehension

The first two paragraphs introduce the topic. Working with a partner, use your own words to discuss what you have learned so far about the Underground Railroad.

neighbor told her how to find the first safe house on her path to freedom. Harriet finally reached the North, where slavery was against the law. She said, "I had crossed the line. I was free; but there was no one to welcome me to the land of freedom. I was a stranger in a strange land."

Harriet's goal became to help those she had left behind. These included her family members. She did not simply enjoy her new freedom. She got a job in Philadelphia. And she saved her money. Harriet returned to Maryland in 1850. She started leading her family to freedom. Over the next ten years, she made the dangerous trip south and back many times. Because of Harriet's work, her family and around seventy other enslaved people escaped. She never "lost" anyone. She never let anyone give up. Harriet was empowered to help these people get to freedom. That's why she carried a gun. She would threaten the people if they became too tired or decided to turn back. When people thought they should quit, she said, "You'll be free or die." She would not accept limitations.

One newspaper in Maryland offered a $100 reward for her capture. But Harriet was priceless to the many people she helped to reach freedom.

Academic Vocabulary

The word *limitation* comes from the root word "limit." What does "limit" mean? How does it help you understand the meaning of *limitation*?

Unlock the Meaning of the Text

Monitor Comprehension Tell a partner the story of Harriet Tubman in your own words. One partner tells about her life before she escaped. One tells about her life after.

Academic Vocabulary The word *empowered* might make you feel strong. What other words make you feel strong? Are these synonyms for *empowered*?

How can ordinary people contribute to a fight for freedom? Make a list of the ways Harriet Tubman helped others find freedom. How can you or people you know help others do the same?

How We Protect Our Freedoms

Academic Vocabulary

An antonym of the word *limitation* is "freedom." How else could you describe the opposite of having *limitations*?

After the Civil War, many states had separate schools for African American children and white children. In these neighborhoods, African American children could not attend the same schools as their white peers. There were many other limitations on when and where African Americans and whites could interact. This was called segregation. Things started to change in 1954 because of a decision by the United States Supreme Court. The Supreme Court is part of one of the three divisions of our government. It is called the judicial branch.

In 1896, the Supreme Court ruled that segregation was legal between white Americans and black Americans. The concept behind the Court's ruling was to keep the two races separate but give them equal opportunities for work and education. Slavery had been outlawed since 1865, shortly after the end of the Civil War. But many citizens still did not believe that African Americans and white Americans should live and work together.

Unfortunately, there was nothing equal about America's schools for black children. Most of the schools were very old. Some didn't have running water or electricity. The textbooks were old and the information in them was no longer correct. Some of the teachers did not have the proper schooling to teach children. The races were separate. But they were not equal.

A man named Oliver Brown decided to resist the idea of "separate but equal." He believed that because African American children were going to segregated schools, they were not getting an equal education. Brown's daughter, Linda, was a third-grade student. They lived in Topeka, Kansas. Linda had to walk many blocks to the school for black children. The school for white children was only a few blocks away from the Browns' home. Oliver Brown felt this was discrimination. Several other parents did, too. They felt empowered to do what was right for their children.

In 1952, the parents first brought their argument to the United States Supreme Court. The Supreme Court decides whether a law is constitutional or not. The Court is in Washington, D.C. There are nine justices on the Court. All nine of the justices agreed that the laws regarding "separate but equal" were unconstitutional. Schools could no longer be segregated by race. Children would be free to go to the school closest to their home.

Sometimes we can stand up for our own rights. But sometimes we need help. One of the jobs of our government is to protect our freedoms. The Supreme Court did its job. Now, all children can get an equal education.

Academic Vocabulary

The prefix re- in the word resist means "to be against." How does knowing this help us define the word resist?

Summarize

Tell a partner, in your own words, what "separate but equal" meant for African Americans in the early 1900s, based on your reading.

Unlock the Meaning of the Text

Summarize After reading the text, work in a small group to summarize the story. What was the problem? What did the people do to solve it?

Academic Vocabulary A synonym for empower means "to feel confident." What details from the text give us clues to how the parents felt empowered?

What can governments do to protect our freedoms? With a partner, identify from the text which freedom the parents were fighting for. Then, discuss why the government needed to help protect their freedom.

She Fought for Women's Rights

Elizabeth Cady Stanton was born in Johnstown, New York, in 1815. Men had much more influence at that time. They had many more options for employment than women in the United States. American women could not become government leaders. Nor could they be preachers or professors. Girls with an interest in public speaking or politics were steered in other directions. Women were not allowed to vote. Elizabeth was expected to have grace. She would be a wife and mother when she grew up like other girls at the time. It was what everyone expected.

It's not surprising that Elizabeth Cady Stanton did become a wife and mother. But Stanton was very interested in politics as well. She worked hard to make slavery against the law in the United States. She did a lot of work for that movement before she got married in 1840. After that, she and her husband went to an antislavery meeting in England.

But Stanton mainly cared about how women were treated. In the mid-1800s, American women didn't have many rights. Women could not serve on a jury. They could not get an equal education. They could not get a divorce. Stanton helped organize the Women's Rights Convention in Seneca Falls, New York, in 1848. She wrote a declaration of women's rights. It was adopted and signed by the people attending the meeting. The declaration demanded that the same rights be given to women and men.

By the 1860s, Stanton was speaking and writing often about the limitations on women. Both men and

Academic Vocabulary

The word *grace* means both "elegance" and "a prayer of thanks." Which meaning best fits the use of *grace* in this sentence?

Academic Vocabulary

The root word of *limitation* is "limit." In Latin, "limit" means "boundary." How does this help you understand the definition of *limitation*?

women disagreed with her. Some made fun of her. Others simply ignored her. Stanton stood strong in her beliefs. She continued to travel a lot. She made speeches and tried to change people's minds.

Stanton disagreed with people on her side, too. Most people who believed in women's rights also believed that African Americans should be given the right to vote. Some politicians wanted to allow black men to vote. But they still didn't want women to vote. Stanton resisted this idea. She would not support voting rights for African American men if women could not vote. Many other women's rights activists disagreed with her. From 1869 to 1890, the women's rights movement was split into two organizations.

Stanton fought for women's rights into her old age. She inspired thousands of Americans. She died in 1902. Eighteen years later the United States approved the Nineteenth Amendment. This recognized women's right to vote.

Generate Questions

After reading this paragraph, how do you think history would have been different had the women's rights movement stayed united?

Unlock the Meaning of the Text

Generate Questions Create a quiz about Elizabeth Cady Stanton. Write 3–5 questions you might ask about her life, her work, and the women's rights movement.

Academic Vocabulary The word *resist* means to fight against something." What were some of the things Elizabeth Cady Stanton resisted?

What are some things people can do when their freedom is limited? With a partner, discuss Elizabeth Cady Stanton's actions when her freedom was limited. What are some things you would do if you were in her situation?

A Better Life in Kansas

Academic Vocabulary

The word *limitations* ends with the suffix *-s*, which makes the word plural. What other plural words can you find in the text?

Jefferson Wilson was born into slavery in the South. Because the North won the Civil War, people expected opportunities for a better life. But the reality was not what they expected. Jefferson Wilson and other former slaves had many limitations. They worked as sharecroppers. It's not surprising they were not happy with life in their Tennessee town.

A white man owned the land that Jefferson Wilson worked. Jefferson's wife and his three sons worked there too. The rent was high and the rates for crops were low. Jefferson's family was always in debt. The same was true for others like him. Living conditions were harsh. Tension between whites and blacks made Jefferson worry for his family's safety.

Academic Vocabulary

One of the antonyms for *empowered* is "enslaved." What other antonyms for *empowered* can you name?

One day, Jefferson walked through Nashville. He spotted an advertisement for moving out to Kansas. A businessman he knew named Benjamin Singleton had posted it. Jefferson researched further. He soon figured out that he could afford transportation for his family. This was only if he didn't buy seeds for another year of planting on the farm. He had long discussions with friends and family. Many of them chose to stay in Tennessee. But the Wilsons felt empowered. They decided to head west with Mr. Singleton and one other family. They were to help establish the all-black community of Dunlap, Kansas. The journey was long and difficult. Yellow fever claimed the lives of several travelers. Hopes of finding new opportunities helped them keep going west.

When the Wilsons arrived, they faced many physical and emotional challenges. Farming in Kansas was hard. They were lonely. There was one thing that really mattered. It was that Jefferson Wilson and his neighbors owned the land they worked. They owned the houses they built. It was theirs. They had problems with discrimination in Kansas. But they no longer lived in constant fear for their lives. They lived a noble life.

The community built its own school. It was called The Dunlap Academy and Mission School. Jefferson Wilson was proud to say his sons went to the school. More and more black families came to Dunlap as time passed. They created a close community of hundreds of families.

The Wilsons had some problems constructing their house and clearing ground to plant. But Jefferson Wilson and his wife never regretted their decision to begin a new life in Kansas. Their crops eventually grew. Life became easier. They had sacrificed a lot to start over. But they knew they had made the right choice for their family. Most importantly, they finally knew what freedom truly meant.

Make Inferences

What can you infer from the information in the fourth paragraph? How was Jefferson's life different in Kansas than in Tennessee?

Unlock the Meaning of the Text

Make Inferences Read the third paragraph. Can you infer why some of Jefferson Wilson's friends and family might want to stay in Tennessee?

Academic Vocabulary Explain in your own words to a partner why owning their own home and land was *noble* for the Wilson family. Use synonyms of the word to help explain your position.

How can going to a new place give a person new opportunities? With a partner, discuss the new opportunities Jefferson was hoping for in Kansas. How can a new place help us find new opportunities?

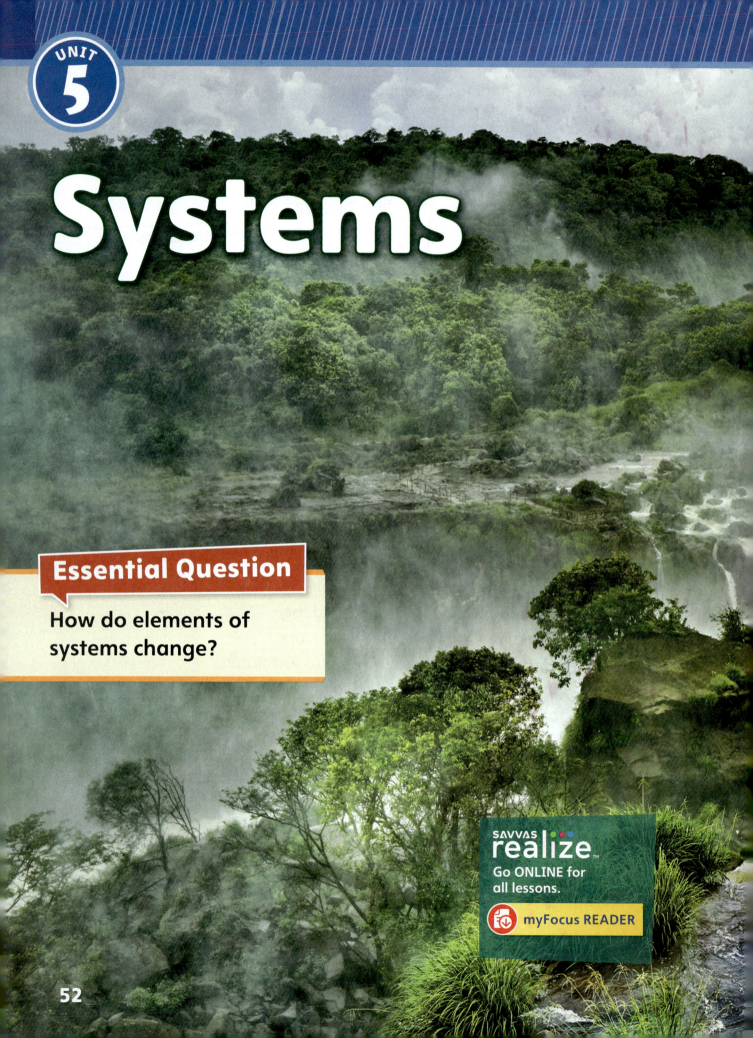

UNIT 5

Systems

Essential Question

How do elements of systems change?

Read and Interact with Text
Develop comprehension and vocabulary. Make connections.

How Do Rocks Change?
Weekly Question How do rocks form and change over time?
Comprehension Main idea
Academic Vocabulary Root words and affixes

How Water Changes Form
Weekly Question What can cause water to change form?
Comprehension Predictions
Academic Vocabulary Part of speech

Struggles and Change for a Small Island Nation
Weekly Question How can Earth's changes affect where and how we live?
Comprehension Inferences
Academic Vocabulary Shades of meaning

Our Impact on the Life Cycle of Fish
Weekly Question How do human actions create and change cycles?
Comprehension Comprehension
Academic Vocabulary Synonyms

Why Is Dog Training Important?
Weekly Question How much should people try to influence natural systems?
Comprehension Connections
Academic Vocabulary Meaning relationships

HOW DO ROCKS CHANGE?

Identify Main Idea and Details

After reading the first two paragraphs, what do you think is the main idea of the text? What details helped you figure that out?

Academic Vocabulary

In this case, the word *composed* means "made up of." What noun does the word *composed* refer to in this sentence?

Take a look at the ground the next time you are outside. If you can, try to find different kinds of rocks. Arrange them side by side. You'll probably notice that some rocks are different from others. Some might be round. Some have sharp edges. Others might be rough or smooth. Some might shine like gold or silver. Some might have many colors. Others might be only one color. No matter how many rocks you have, there's a good chance those rocks have been around for a long time. They have also changed forms many times since they were first created.

Living things like plants and animals have a life cycle. They are born, grow up, and then die. But did you know rocks have a life cycle, too? Depending on where they are formed and the environment where they are, rocks can change.

There are three main kinds of rock on Earth: igneous, sedimentary, and metamorphic. All three of these kinds of rocks come from magma, the lava that flows from volcanoes. Magma is composed of minerals. When magma cools, it forms igneous rock. Some examples of igneous rocks are obsidian and granite. You might have kitchen counters at home that are granite.

Igneous rock that cools quickly forms tiny grains of sand. The sand can travel to new places in the wind. Sometimes, the sand will travel far away from where the first rock was formed. Bits of sand can come together after a long time and join together. These form sedimentary rocks. These rocks are popular for building homes and walls. Limestone, slate, and sandstone are all sedimentary rocks.

Metamorphic rocks are formed from the impact of heat and pressure on igneous rock. These are some of the hardest rocks on Earth. Sometimes metamorphic rocks have stripes. The stripes show what kinds of minerals are in the rock. Marble and quartz are examples of metamorphic rocks.

The cycle continues as Earth's crust moves around. As it disturbs the surface, it might break up and wash away some of the metamorphic rock. Magma can flow from newly formed volcanoes and new igneous rocks are created. Then, the life cycle of the rock starts over.

Academic Vocabulary

The word *impact* means both "come into contact" and "have a strong effect." Which meaning best fits the use of the word in this sentence?

Unlock the Meaning of the Text

Identify Main Idea and Details With a partner, list all the details in the text that describe different kinds of rocks. Then, identify the names of each rock.

Academic Vocabulary The word *disturb* comes from the Latin root "turba," which means "disorder." How does knowing this help us figure out the meaning of *disturb*?

How do rocks form and change over time? In a small group, write down the steps in the rock cycle. Put them in order. Then, discuss the cycle in your own words.

How Water Changes Form

The most vital thing that makes Earth unique is water. Because Earth has water, plants and animals can live here. Humans can exist on Earth only because there is water. Our bodies are composed of 60 percent water. Earth's surface is only about 30 percent land. The majority of the planet is water. Water encompasses us. It's the air we breathe, what we drink, and the ice that cools our drinks. The water cycle is what keeps our planet healthy and flourishing.

Make and Confirm Predictions

With a partner, write down the three states of water. Then make predictions about how one state becomes another based on the reading.

Contrary to what you might think, though, water isn't where the cycle begins. We have a water cycle because of the sun. Other planets in our solar system have ice, but because they are too far from the sun, that ice will never melt and become water. Earth is unique. We are exactly far enough away from the sun to have ice, water, and vapor. These are the three "states" of water.

Let's begin with the oceans. The sun heats the water in the oceans, and the water evaporates. It becomes known as water vapor, which is a gas. Some of the water vapor is in the air we breathe. When it is hot and sticky outside, it is humid. That means there is more water vapor in the air than usual. When it is very dry, there is less water vapor in the air. Other water vapor rises to the sky and forms cirrus, cumulus, stratus, or other types of clouds. When the clouds become saturated with water vapor, it rains.

However, if the air is very cold, the clouds might not rain liquid water. Ice, the solid state of water, can form. Ice is **composed** of liquid water and air. Depending on the temperature, the water could freeze into crystals and fall as snow. Or, if the temperature is not quite cold enough to freeze, it could sleet. When very large droplets of water combine and freeze in the air, that will form masses of ice called hail.

When frozen water reaches the ground, it eventually melts and runs off into the soil for plants and animals. Plants release water vapor from their leaves. Animals drink from ponds, rivers, and lakes when rain runs down to the lowest point of the area.

Some of the water drains underground and gathers in the spaces between rocks and soil. Spaces totally filled with water are called *aquifers*. Aquifers can store groundwater for long periods of time. The process starts again. Earth is **engineered** to be sustainable if we take care of it.

Academic Vocabulary

The word *composed* means "made up of." In this sentence, what two nouns does the verb *composed* refer to.

Academic Vocabulary

The word *engineered* is from the Latin root *ingeniare*, which means "to come up with." How does knowing this help you learn the meaning of *engineer*?

Unlock the Meaning of the Text

Make and Confirm Predictions After reading the last sentence, discuss what might happen if we don't care for Earth. What will happen to the plants, animals, and humans?

Academic Vocabulary The word *cycle* is both a noun and a verb. Which part of speech is used for the word *cycle* in the first paragraph?

What can cause water to change form? In a small group, discuss the three states of water. What makes each stage change form? What stages of water have you seen today?

Struggles and Change for a Small Island Nation

How would things be different if your whole country were only a third of the size of Manhattan in New York City? What about a tenth of the size of Washington, D.C.? The Republic of Nauru (nah-OO-roo) is just that. The whole country is just 8.1 square miles (21 square km)! The island is located just south of the equator in the southern Pacific Ocean. Nauru is the world's smallest island nation. About twelve thousand people live there.

Even though there are warm temperatures and beautiful sandy beaches on Naurau, the residents face serious problems. For example, no one can live in the middle 80 percent of the island. Nauruans (nah-OO-roo-inz) crowd together on a narrow strip of land that runs along the beach.

What happened to the land in the middle? For one hundred years, people mined the land. The small country made a lot of money. But mining disturbed the environment. The president of Nauru has said mining cleared the tropical rainforest that once covered the middle of the island. It impacted the land.

Another problem is the lack of fresh water. This is the kind of water needed for drinking. The houses in Nauru have roof storage tanks to collect rain. But

Academic Vocabulary

The word *disturb* means "to make anxious" or "to interrupt normal function." Which meaning best fits this sentence with the word *disturb*?

58

most people rely on a desalination plant for their water. The desalination plant uses a cycle to remove salt from the ocean water to make it drinkable. But the plant is old and there is only one on the island.

Now, there are few natural resources. Most people are poor. Those who do have jobs work mainly for the government or in mines. Others raise coconuts or fish. Little fertile land remains.

Nauru is more than 185 miles from its nearest neighbor, Ocean Island. It's hard to import food and other necessities. Foreign countries send the island nation money to survive. A seaport cannot be built because the island is surrounded by a tall coral reef. There is only one main road and one airport. Travel on the island can be hard.

Opportunities for education and health care are also limited. The average person goes to school for only nine years. Residents also have limited access to television and radio. Both are run by the government. Most people are overweight. There are only a few doctors. Nauruans face terrible problems. They don't want to give up their little nation. So, it will take a lot of time, education, determination, and help to make life better.

Academic Vocabulary
The word *cycle* is both a noun and a verb. Which part of speech makes the most sense for this use of the word *cycle*?

Make Inferences
After reading the text, what can you infer about the people of Nauru? Why do they value their island? Why don't they leave?

Unlock the Meaning of the Text

Make Inferences Read the third paragraph. What can you infer about the impact of mining on the island? What were the good and bad things about it?

Academic Vocabulary The word *impact* means both "an effect or influence" and "to press firmly." Which is the meaning that fits best in the third paragraph?

How can Earth's changes affect where and how we live? In a group, write down the environmental challenges the Nauruans face. How do changes in Earth affect where and how we live?

Our Impact on the Life Cycle of Fish

The Columbia River flows to the west for more than 1,200 miles (1,931 kilometers). The river runs across the northwest United States. Sounds like a paradise for fish, right? It was at one time, until humans decided to control the water flowing to the ocean. No one asked the fish what they thought.

A dam is a structure built by humans across a river. Dams help prevent floods. They also provide water for farms. Larger dams make clean and cheap power. More than four hundred dams have been built along the Columbia River over time. Eleven of them run the whole way across the river.

But think about how these dams impact the natural environment. Think about the salmon's life cycle. Salmon make only two long trips during their lives. They hatch in rivers far from the ocean. Then, young salmon swim to the ocean where they spend their adult lives. They swim back to where they were hatched before they die. In the cool streams, females lay eggs, and males fertilize them.

What happens when a young fish swimming toward the ocean comes across a dam that crosses the entire river? Water stored behind the dam rushes down. It travels through tunnels and turns huge propellers to generate electricity. Spinning blades are not a healthy environment for fish!

Academic Vocabulary

The word *cycle* comes from the Greek word "kuklos," which means "circle." How does knowing that help you understand the meaning of the word *cycle*?

Monitor Comprehension

With a partner, take turns explaining how a dam works in your own words based on the reading.

Imagine if the fish somehow makes it to the ocean. Then, it has to return to the river, swimming against the current to reach the place where it was hatched. Fish can do this for long distances when the slope is gentle. But climbing a dam more than 100 feet (30 meters) high is quite a challenge! Dams make it hard for fish to lay eggs. So the numbers of salmon and trout along the Columbia River have dropped from 16 million to 2.5 million.

Builders have **engineered** "fishways," such as fish ladders, in dams since the 1930s. A fish ladder is a series of pools. They slowly go up the dam. These pools are filled with rushing water. The fish swim upriver against the current. They leap from a lower pool to a higher one. They rest in the pool, then they repeat the process until they are above the dam.

Fish ladders are like elevators. They fill with fish, then they rise to the top of the dam and open to let the fish out. They can add millions of dollars to a dam's cost. Do you think the cost is worth it? Causing whole species of fish to die is **disturbing**. Preserving the environment is priceless.

Academic Vocabulary

The word *engineer* is both a noun and a verb. Which part of speech is *engineer* in the first sentence of the sixth paragraph?

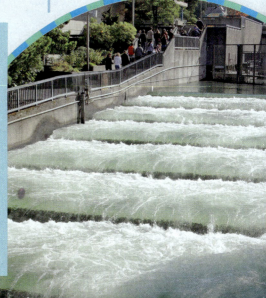

Unlock the Meaning of the Text

Monitor Comprehension Write the steps in the life cycle of a salmon in a circle using details from the text. Why is it called a life *cycle*?

Academic Vocabulary A meaning for the word *disturbing* is "to cause worry." A synonym is "worrying." What other synonyms can you name for *disturbing*?

How do human actions create and change cycles? In a group, discuss the impact the dams made on the fish. Then, discuss the changes humans made for the fish. How do our actions create and change cycles in nature?

Why Is Dog Training Important?

Academic Vocabulary

The word *disturbed* has a negative connotation. How does knowing that help you understand the first paragraph better?

It shouldn't be astonishing to dog owners that some people do not like being around dogs. Sometimes unsupervised, unleashed dogs sniff around, bark at, or jump on people. Some naive dog owners actually smile with pride. They may even coo a few phrases of love or praise for their four-legged, furry friends. There's something even worse. Sometimes the owners are disturbed that someone might not love their precious pooch's antics. An untrained dog is not nice to be around. Dog owners need to understand that dogs both want and need training.

The first reason to train a dog is that it wants to be trained. Dogs are descended from wolves. They understand and love the pack mentality. In wolf packs, one of the wolves is the leader. This is also called the alpha. Many obedience classes help a dog owner learn to be the alpha. Through a cycle of praise and rewards, dogs can be taught to sit, stay, and come when their owners command. The owners need a lot of patience. Dogs do still need some time to run and play freely on their own, of course. But, in general, you should be the leader. Your pet should be the follower.

Academic Vocabulary

The word *composed* is used here as an adjective. Identify the word in the sentence that the adjective *composed* describes.

Training dogs is good for other reasons, too. You may no longer be able take care of your dog one day. The chances of your dog being placed a new home are better if your dog is trained and composed. Other people are also likely to be less fearful and act more friendly and welcoming toward your dog. But they need to be sure the animal is under your control. Your pet will bask in the extra interaction. It will love the attention it gets from others.

Finally, training your dog might even save its life at some point. An untrained and disobedient dog may run off when a door is inadvertently left open. It might come back when it feels like it. Or it might not come back at all. But a trained dog can be called back to you promptly. This can avoid it being hit by a vehicle. The effort you put into training will also pay off when you take your dog for a walk. Trained dogs cross streets more safely. They know to stay by your side and will obey your commands. They will be far less likely to be distracted by traffic or another animal.

Do right by your dog and get it trained. You'll quickly notice how others will enjoy being around your dog, too.

Make Connections
What connections can you make between having a trained dog or untrained dog and how people react to your pet?

Unlock the Meaning of the Text

Make Connections After reading the second paragraph, what connection can you make between dogs and their ancestors, the wolves? How does that affect the dog's behavior?

Academic Vocabulary The word *cycle* refers to the events in a training session. Explain how to train a dog in your own words without using the word *cycle*.

How much should people try to influence natural systems? With a partner, explain a dog's natural behavior based on your reading. How is the training helping or hurting that natural behavior?

Acknowledgments

Photographs

Photo locators denoted as follows Top (T), Center (C), Bottom (B), Left (L), Right (R), Background (Bkgd)

4 I Love Photo/Shutterstock, **6** (B) Andrii IURLOV/123RF, (BR) Torsten Blackwood/Getty Images, **8** (Bkgrd) Lucia Pitter/Shutterstock, (TR) Royal Photographic Society, **10** (Bkgrd) Belikova/123RF, (BL) Brand X Pictures/Thinkstock/Getty Images, **12** (BL) Organica/Alamy Stock Photo, (TR) Library of Congress Prints and Photographs Division Washington, D.C. 20540, Reproduction Number: LC-USZ62-20319, **14** (Bkgrd) Luba Shushpanova/Fotolia, (CR) Wajan/Fotolia, (R) Fotolia, (TR) Zedu/Fotolia, **16** ESB Professional/Shutterstock, **18** (Bkgrd) John Anderson/Fotolia, (TR) NASA, **19** Paul Shawcross/Alamy Stock Photo, **20** (Bkgrd) Uryadnikov Sergey/Fotolia, (BL) Runolfur/Fotolia, (TR) Uryadnikov Sergey/Fotolia, **22** (Bkgrd) Thinkstock/Getty Images, (BL) BGSmith/Shutterstock, (T) Magnum/Fotolia, **23** Cuson/Shutterstock, **24** (Bkgrd) Piotr Krzeslak/Shutterstock, (TL) akhug//Fotolia, **25** (BR) Paul837/Fotolia, (TR) Davy Hiller/Fotolia, **26** Krofoto/Shutterstock, **27** Macdivers/Fotolia, **28** David Pereiras/Shuttestock, **30** (Bkgrd) Library of Congress Prints and Photographs Division Washington, D.C. 20540, Reproduction Number: LC-DIG-ppbd-00358, **31** (CR) WENN/Newscom, (R) Library of Congress Prints and Photographs Division Washington, D.C. 20540, Reproduction Number: LC-DIG-ppmsca-04296, **32** (Bkgrd) Ryan McVay/Thinkstock/Getty Images, (CR) SOTK2011/Alamy Stock Photo, **33** Jure Porenta/Shutterstock, **34** (B) Stefanos Kyriazis/Fotolia, (T) Gary Blakeley/Fotolia, **35** Dmitry Erashov/Fotolia, **36** (BR) Monart Design/Fotolia, (L) Andy Dean/Fotolia, **37** (L) Aberenyi/Fotolia, (R) Thinkstock/Getty Images, **38** (B) Hemera Technologies/Thinkstock/Getty Images, (T) Smithsonian American Art Museum, Washington, DC/Art Resource, NY, **39** (C) Hemera Technologies/Thinkstock/Getty Images, (R) Klavlav4ik/Fotolia, **40** Russell Kord/Alamy Stock Photo, **42** (Bkgrd) Fotolia, (TR) Hemera Technologies/Thinkstock/Getty Images, **43** Martin Zavala/Xinhua/Sipa Press/Newscom, **44** (Bkgrd) Fotolia, (C) David M Schrader/Fotolia, (TR) Thinkstock/Getty Images, **45** (BR) IMAGINE/Fotolia, (TR) Library of Congress Prints and Photographs Division Washington, D.C. 20540, Reproduction Number: LC-USZ62-7816; **46** Gary Blakeley/Shutterstock, **47** Everett Collection Historical Alamy Stock Photo, **48** (Bkgrd) Fotolia, (B) Thinkstock/Getty Images, (TL) Library of Congress Prints and Photographs Division Washington, D.C. 20540, Reproduction Number: LC-USZ62-48965, **50** (Bkgrd) Ryan McVay/Thinkstock/Getty Images, (TR) Everett Collection Inc/Alamy Stock Photo, **51** Library of Congress Prints and Photographs Division Washington, D.C. 20540, Reproduction Number: HABS KANS,33-NICO,1–6, **52** Aleksandra H. Kossowska/Shutterstock, **54** (Bkgrd) I WALL/Shutterstock, (BL) Tyler Boyes/Shutterstock, **55** Oreena/Shutterstock, **56** (Bkgrd) Ratana21/Shutterstock, (CL) Creative Travel Projects/Shutterstock, (TR) Kevin Eaves/Shutterstock, **57** 2009fotofriends/Shutterstock, **58** Maria Skaldina/Fotolia, **60** (Bkgrd) Hemera Technologies/Thinkstock/Getty Images, (CR) TFoxFoto/Shutterstock, (TL) Jennifer Buchanan/123RF, **61** Rigucci/Shutterstock, **62** M.studio/Fotolia, **63** lightpoet/Fotolia.